This book belongs to:

____

38510981R00061

Made in the USA
Lexington, KY
08 May 2019